Coffee and Jesus
Morning Devotions of Encouragement

Author: Andrea Kellum

Dedication

This book is dedicated to the beautiful ladies of Coffee and Jesus for always sharing your wisdom with me. I appreciate your love and your constant encouragement. I am humbled and honored to worship Jesus with you every morning! You are brave! You are bold! You are enough! You are worthy! You are loved!

About the Author

Andrea Kellum is the founder of Changing Crowns Ministries, a former internationally recognized pageant coach, national pageant titleholder, worship leader, author, speaker, and homeschool mom. She has been married for 15 years to Jeremy Kellum and they reside in Woodstock, Alabama, along with their teenage son, Kainen.

Andrea passionately serves women in her community and around the world as a teacher of WAR night at The Refreshing Place Church and as the founder of Coffee and Jesus; a live daily devotional group for more than 4,000 women from every state in America and over 33 countries worldwide.

Her desire is to help women better understand God's word, to encourage them to find their identity in Christ and to love women in Christ-like ways that bond all Christian women in a unified, and strongly knit together community. Andrea hopes to use her ministry in a manner that teaches women to embrace every intricate part of their individual purpose in Christ.

Contents

Introduction

During the spring of 2017, I began to crave the wisdom of God like never before. I knew there was something happening that would cause me to seek after Him with my whole heart. After months of intense physical and spiritual battles, I knew the Lord was calling me to lead women to Jesus. I knew what He asked of me and for weeks (probably months) I fought Him.

After experiencing the most sickening feeling in my stomach for days for not obeying, I caved. I did what God asked me to do and that was to start a women's ministry on facebook to write devotions and share my passion of studying God's word! Coffee and Jesus devotion group was birthed! Since September 4, 2017, I have shared the devotions and studies God has placed on my heart with women across the globe.

There are days I struggle with waking up extra early to study and to be honest I want to stay in my warm bed and sleep. There are days I want to quit because I feel inadequate to be sharing God's word. There are days I want to delete my entire account because my personal struggles consume me, and I can't bear facing these ladies with tears in my eyes. But I know that God has called me to do a task He is qualifying me for.

I can't do this. But He alone can.

There's nothing special that I've done in my life to have the skills or qualifications that I need to lead this. But God does!

I am not someone who most would consider knowledgeable in God's word. But God most certainly is, after all, it's His Word! What started from an act of obedience has turned into something that can only point to Jesus Christ. I thought when this all started there would be maybe 20, give or take, of my closest family and friends joining me each weekday to hear God's message. Little did I know, God had other plans; plans much bigger than I ever imagined.

Today, there are more than 4100 women in Coffee and Jesus, every single state in the USA and 33 countries are represented! WHOA! This is insane! This is God in action! There's nothing I could possibly do to create this! I'm merely a little country gal from Woodstock, Alabama! But My God is powerful! He is wonderful! He is plentiful! He provides! He knows all! He is faithful! God is so, so good!

If He is telling you to make a move, then Do It! Now! Don't worry with what everyone else thinks or what they will say! Allow God to move before you in His calling and trust that He WILL provide for you, and YOU be certain everything you do points people to Jesus! Thank you, Father, for being so gracious to me! The enemy has tried to stop me many times during these past few months, but I am strong and ONLY BECAUSE OF JESUS CHRIST! Jesus Christ is my everything!

"so My word that comes from My mouth will not return to Me empty, but it will accomplish what I please and will prosper in what I send it to do.""
Isaiah 55:11 HCSB

"Go, therefore, and make disciples of all nations, baptizing them in the name of the Father and of the Son and of the Holy Spirit,"
Matthew 28:19 HCSB

"For nothing will be impossible with God.""
Luke 1:37 HCSB

Don't Ignore Him

You know those moments you hear God whisper to you? Not an audible whisper, but a whisper to your heart that you are sure is Him tugging you into the direction He needs you? That's where I've been. I tried to ignore Him. For a Very. Long. Time. Then I realized I must share the words He speaks to me to send His message to others. His message. Not my own. The message that no matter where you are in life or who you are surrounded by, He purposely placed you here for a reason. He designed you with desires in your heart. He built you with all the essential tools you would need to know what your job for Him is, so you can accomplish it.

This is my job. To help you reach yours. To help you fully understand that you can and will. You have been crafted, created, and perfectly stitched together with everything you need.

Today, you need to accept that as truth. The truth that all those people who say you can't are wrong, because He says you can! The truth that all those times you are told no, is because someone better is going to say yes. The truth that when you cling to Him for your contentment and fulfillment He will provide. That's the truth. You see, this message you are reading is because

He connected our lives for purpose and beauty. If our connection is only meant for this one message, take it in with all your heart and focus on the greatness He has given you. Embrace the beauty of you. Because you, my friend, YOU were created for much more than you can imagine.

Colossians 1:16

All About Me

Are we missing out on blessing others around us? Christmas time always brings about the giving heart we each have in us. We give to our favorite charities, we give to families in need, to the homeless, to children who may not wake up Christmas morning with gifts; the list goes on and on.

While all of these things are wonderful, and I fully believe are beneficial, God has placed on my heart that my personal giving should go further than these normal things. We think about giving most often of things such as money or material possessions. But how much more do we have that we aren't giving?

What about the lady you see struggling in the grocery store; coupons in hand, children crying, trying to check off her list and keep her sanity! Could you give her a word of encouragement? Or the homeless man sitting on the corner near your workplace, who just gets tossed a few dollars or coins each day; maybe you've given to him as well; but have you stopped and prayed with him? Maybe he simply needs friendship today. At church you see a lady who is quiet, never says much, but is always there when the doors open. You acknowledge her with a hello each time, but maybe she needs to hear that God loves her and she is important!

Have you told her that lately? We could list hundreds of scenarios, but I believe you see the point. How many of God's children are we walking by day after day and not truly blessing? We get so caught up in ourselves and our excuses that we sometimes forget there are people, God's people, hurting around us.

"I'm tired."

"I'll be late if I stop today."

"I'll just say a prayer instead of talking to her."

"I don't have enough for myself to be giving what I do have away."

"I'm scared others will laugh."

Do any of these statements sound familiar to you? They did to me! Hugs, prayers, a smile, encouragement, time: those are all things God has spoken to me as reminders of how much more I truly can give to His children! Let's open our eyes to those around us; let's be the hands and feet of Jesus, not just in giving from our pocketbooks and wallets, but giving in ALL we have.

"If anyone has this world's goods and sees his brother in need but closes his eyes to his need — how can God's love reside in him?"
1 John 3:17 HCSB

"Everyone should look out not only for his own interests, but also for the interests of others."
Philippians 2:4 HCSB

12

<u>Studied</u>

I've been studying the lives of the 12 disciples this month with my Coffee and Jesus ladies. It's got me thinking about a few things...

You see with each person we study, we look at a few topics in their lives: their occupation, their most obvious characteristics (not all of them are exemplary), what Jesus spoke to them, who their families were, what the most significant moment of their life was, and even how they died for Jesus Christ.

Sometimes we walk about our daily lives, doing normal things, not thinking too much about what it may look like to others, but as a Christ follower, we are to be as much like Him as possible. These 12 disciples had the privilege of walking with our Lord and Savior in the flesh and yet they still failed. Some of them turned their back on Him, denied Him; some were at times impulsive or greedy; and although they each had very great qualities about them, they also had very human actions as well. Then I was intrigued by these questions:

What if someone decided to study me? What would they see? What would my outstanding characteristics be? What would my failures teach others? What has Jesus said to me that impacted someone else?

We may not walk with Jesus in the flesh, but we can walk daily with Him, talking and listening to His guidance through the Holy Spirit. I want to ask you the same tough questions I asked myself.

What if someone decided to study your life?
Would they call you a disciple of Jesus?

"My sheep hear My voice, I know them, and they follow Me." John 10:27

The Formula of Success

When God called upon Joshua after the death of Moses He spoke words of encouragement to Joshua.

""6. Be strong and courageous, for you will distribute the land I swore to their fathers to give them as an inheritance. 7. Above all, be strong and very courageous to carefully observe the whole instruction My servant Moses commanded you. Do not turn from it to the right or the left, so that you will have success wherever you go. 8. This book of instruction must not depart from your mouth; you are to recite it day and night so that you may carefully observe everything written in it. For then you will prosper and succeed in whatever you do. 9. Haven't I commanded you: be strong and courageous? Do not be afraid or discouraged, for the Lord your God is with you wherever you go.""

Joshua 1:6-9 HCSB

Within this set of scriptures our Almighty, Powerful God spoke a command to Joshua again and again. The command given was, "Be strong and courageous".

So often I have read these scriptures and applied them to my own personal situations; especially in times of doubt.

But what I have obviously overlooked sits perfectly situated within these words from God. Look at verses

7-8. How many times do we hear verse 9 and overlook the rest.

God didn't only command Joshua to be strong and courageous, He gave him the exact formula of success that he would need to follow the command. It's right in the center of the obvious!

In order for Joshua to know God's commands sent through His servant Moses, in order for Joshua to know how to remain strong and courageous, in order for Joshua to know God's promises to His people, Joshua must recite God's word, carefully observe it, not turn to the right or the left from it and THEN he will prosper and succeed. So many times, in our lives, we want to fix the broken things, we want to correct the wrongs, we want to have what the world sees as success and we can be easily thrown off the path of God's plan for us because of this.

Thankfully, we have an incredible Heavenly Father who loves us and reminds us within His Word, within the Holy Bible, the exact success formula needed.

Are you struggling with not seeing success in your life? God's success and the world's success are much different from one another, and God's success is much greater than any worldly success can offer you.

Open your bible, begin to read God's word, recite it day and night, and find success in the eyes of God within His scriptures.

Be strong and courageous, friends.

The Purest Heart

Every year at Christmas Jeremy, Kainen and I choose a new ornament. Usually it is something that represents that year for us; an accomplishment we've had or a hobby we love.

"But the Lord said to Samuel, "Do not look at his appearance or his stature, because I have rejected him. Man does not see what the Lord sees, for man sees what is visible, but the Lord sees the heart.""
1 Samuel 16:7 HCSB

A few days ago, while we were selecting our tree for this year, Kainen asked me if we could each have a scripture ornament; on our ornaments would have each of our favorite scriptures. As he told me his and then asked what mine would be, the above scripture came to mind. It's the scripture I used in my pageantry business to teach my clients many lessons about winning with humility. I was reading this scripture today and I thought of the many lessons within this story.

See Samuel was searching for the anointed one, the chosen one to replace Saul as king. God had rejected Saul because of his disobedience. Saul had become more concerned with what others thought of him than with his relationship with God.

When Samuel was sent to Jesse of Bethlehem, he may have expected to find the new king to be someone of great looks and height; someone who may have resembled the outward appearance of King Saul. However, very quickly he learned that God wasn't searching for great looks. He was searching for a great heart.

Samuel wonders if Eliab, the first of Jesse's sons to be mentioned, was the anointed one. I imagine that his appearance was most likely one of great stature because of what God says to Samuel in verse 7. Then follows Abinadab, Shammah, and the remaining of the sons, but none of them are the chosen one. The Bible doesn't give us much more description of these sons and their appearances. But what God's word does focus on and gives us are a few key points about the one who was chosen by God to be anointed. David. Shepherd boy, David. The youngest. Possibly the smallest of the brothers. We know that he is described to have a healthy and handsome appearance, but again, God doesn't require this in his choosing.

He is concerned with the heart; humility, obedience, submission. Those are the characteristics of the anointed one. As I read God's message within these scriptures it also reminds me of the birth of our Lord Jesus Christ! How humble He came, how obedient to our Father He was, and even when He knew there was

21

no other way but death, how submissive He was to give His life for us. Let's be reminded that what our eyes are able to gaze upon is not what our Lord is seeking from us. It is our heart. Our purest, loving and humble heart. That is what God desires in His chosen people.

O Holy Night

O holy night has always been my absolute favorite Christmas song. It embodies everything that Christmas should be about; the remembrance of Christ's birth, the sinful world awaiting the arrival of a Savior, a King sent with message of hope, peace, and love.

"We love because He first loved us."
1 John 4:19 HCSB

Reading the birth of Jesus in the scriptures, I have often tried to imagine myself present in that moment. What would it feel like to be in the presence of the newborn King? How beautiful would it be to see all the heavenly hosts rejoice?

Can we even begin to imagine those things?

I want to share some of the words of "O Holy Night" with you, but as you read these next few lines let them sink in. Really, soak in them for a moment.

"Truly He taught us to love one another, His law is love and His gospel is peace."

Love and peace. That's what Jesus taught us. From His long-awaited arrival to His final breath on earth. Love and peace.

If we will begin to uncover the layers of wrapping paper, decorations, traffic, the tree trimming, and the hustle and bustle from one holiday gathering to the next, then and only then will we find the true Christmas meaning. The reason we have designated this day of celebration, Jesus Christ. Doesn't He deserve a celebration of praise daily?

Love and peace to each of you. May Jesus be the star that brightens your Christmas this year.

"Chains He shall break, for the slave is our brother. And in His name all oppression shall cease. Sweet hymns of joy in grateful chorus raise we, with all our hearts we praise His holy name. Christ is the Lord! Then ever, ever praise we, His power and glory ever more proclaim! His power and glory ever more proclaim!"

Woman with Purpose

So many women in the Bible have impacted my walk with Christ. The woman at the well, the adulterous woman, Mary and Martha, I could name them all and with each one I could list a million lessons I've learned because of them.

Esther has always been one of my favorite women to study. I think mostly because she was a queen, something I could easily connect with in my previous industry of pageantry. But over the past few months, I have come to have a new-found love for the study of Anna, the prophetess. We don't know very many things about her. She doesn't have a book named after her, not even a few chapters. All she has for us to study her are 3 scriptures mentioning her life.

"There was also a prophetess, Anna, a daughter of Phanuel, of the tribe of Asher. She was well along in years, having lived with her husband seven years after her marriage, and was a widow for 84 years. She did not leave the temple complex, serving God night and day with fasting and prayers. At that very moment, she came up and began to thank God and to speak about Him to all who were looking forward to the redemption of Jerusalem."
Luke 2:36-38 HCSB

27

We know from these scriptures that she was the daughter of Phanuel, of the tribe of Asher. She had been married, but not very long and then became widowed. But the most important fact that we can learn from her is she spent her life serving God, day and night, with fasting and prayers. Her entire life was spent in the temple complex serving. Scripture doesn't say she lived there waiting for the church to care for because she was widowed, expecting a handout. She served. She had a servant's heart. Scripture doesn't tell us that she wasted her time with the "busy"ness of life, it says she spent her days and nights fasting and praying.

She spent her life devoted to serving God and when He was present before her she recognized Christ and shared about His offer of redemption to everyone.

What a woman! What a mighty, Godly woman! So many lessons within this small amount of information. As I was reminded of her again today, these questions also came to mind; "Would I recognize Jesus?"

"Do I devote myself into studying, praying and fasting enough that I would recognize Jesus?"

My prayer is that each of us will be so open and willing to serving God, day and night, fasting and praying, that when in little moments or large moments, God reveals Himself to us, we will recognize and know Him! God give me a heart willing to serve you at all times!

Focused

We may often find ourselves in moments where it is hard to remain focused on God's promises, and the mission we have all been called to as believers in Christ.

As I read the above scriptures I thought of Noah and how he must have felt. He knew the promises God had made to him, he also knew the mission. And while so many around him could have possibly chosen to make a mockery of him, he never lost focus of what God had commanded of him. Now, the Bible doesn't tell us about the reaction of the people while Noah built the ark but imagine what would it be like if a modern-day Noah was told to build an ark for God. Media outlets would have a field day! He would be talked about, giggled at, and probably by many of us who profess to be believers and followers of Jesus Christ.

Focus.
The center of activity.
To pay particular attention to.

When our everyday lives are filled with calendars and schedules, work and school, spouses and children, it can be difficult to not be distracted and to not lose our focus on what God is asking of us; what He has called each of us to do.

30

It's easy to let the day pass by without reading our bibles. It's easy to say, "I'll catch up on my devotions tomorrow." It's easy for us to 'put off' God.

There's a saying, "Out of Sight, Out of Mind"

It's true in many situations. But it shouldn't be true in this scenario.

God wants to see your mind focused. Focused on Him. On praising Him, on worshipping Him, on praying and speaking to Him.

Not Him being last on your to do list, distracted by people's opinions, your family, your career or even your ministry. He needs and desires for you to have alone time, intimate one on one time with Him.

Don't let the world around and the afflictions you face distract you from the mission God has called you to! What we see is temporary. What God sees is eternal.

Focus, my friend, focus!

"Therefore we do not give up. Even though our outer person is being destroyed, our inner person is being renewed day by day. For our momentary light affliction is producing for us an absolutely incomparable eternal weight of glory. So we do not focus on what is seen, but on what is unseen. For what is seen is temporary, but what is unseen is eternal."
2 Corinthians 4:16-18 HCSB

The Fourth One

It took boldness and courage for these three to walk in faith. Shadrach, Meshach, and Abednego denied bowing to any other god, but the Holy, Almighty, Lord of All! Yahweh, The Great I Am!

They knew that no matter what they faced; whether fire or death or miraculous salvation, their God was with them; they would praise Him only.

Then after the furnace was heated seven times greater than normal, as things began to get really hot, so hot that the men throwing them in were burned up, these three were tossed inside to die!

But what happens next is where you and I can have hope!

The Bible says that King Nebuchadnezzar looks into the furnace and sees not only the three but one more. A fourth person. Jesus.

"He exclaimed, "Look! I see four men, not tied, walking around in the fire unharmed; and the fourth looks like a son of the gods.""
Daniel 3:25 HCSB

Jesus was with them in the midst of the fire. While the one seated on the earthly throne was watching and waiting upon their destruction, there was Jesus, protecting them from the flames.

So greatly protected that not only did these men escape burns, but nothing of them smelled like fire!

As we come to the end of another year, and we each begin to reflect on what happened in the last, how things changed for the good or the bad, whether we met our own accomplishments and goals or if we still have a few to work on, I've pondered on many of these things in my own life the last few days and I found one common factor. Jesus.

Jesus is the thread that is woven within all of my joys, my disappointments, my accomplishments, my fears, my failures, my pains, and my pleasures of 2017.

He's the steady. The constant. The always. The only one I can consistently rely on to have my back, to fight for me, to carry my heavy load, to take my cares.

Sister, I have no idea what your life was like in the past year. I don't know your secrets, I don't know your trials, I don't know what your heart has battled. But I know that whether you realized it or not, Jesus knows, He was there with you and He is ready to be there with you in the new year too!

He is everlasting! Never changing! Always accepting!

If you are about to walk into a new year with burdens, fears, extra baggage, I urge and encourage you with all the love I possibly can hold, lay it all at the feet of Jesus.

Ask for forgiveness. Seek Him first. Ask Him to be the Savior of your life! Acknowledge Him! Accept Him! And lay it all at His feet!

Praise Him in all fires you face!
Walk with Him; Even if!
This will be a year of promises fulfilled if you will only accept the Savior who seeks after your heart!

Won't you cry out to Him today?
Won't you let Him save you from the fire?

May God bless you in this new year!
May God give you a heart willing and hoping for what pleases Him most of all!
May God lead you to His will and His way!

A Joyful Beginning

Today begins our new year.
      New memories, new goals, new intentions.

"God, create a clean heart for me and renew a steadfast spirit within me. Do not banish me from Your presence or take Your Holy Spirit from me. Restore the joy of Your salvation to me, and give me a willing spirit."
Psalms 51:10-12 HCSB

As we each make our plans for the new year, we will not toss aside the memories that may cause many of us to feel we have failed time and time again. But today I want you to begin this new year, this "clean slate" with a reminder of encouragement...

My favorite part of the scriptures above says "restore the JOY of Your salvation"
It takes me back to the moment I finally surrendered my life to Jesus. That first day of a new me! The old me was covered in the precious blood of Jesus and my sins were washed away!

A clean slate!
A new day!
A new life!

I was free, and I was full of joy! Boy, oh boy, full of joy! I was so filled with excitement for this new creation I had just become because of Jesus Christ that I couldn't possibly contain it inside my little body!

I wanted to explode with celebration!

I wanted to tell EVERYONE what I had just experienced!

It was an unspeakable, never before experienced happiness that filled my soul!

But as time passed by those feelings faded.

I quickly learned not everyone was as thrilled as I was. It started to become clear to me that there would be times only I would feel this joy and that others on this journey may not.

There would be times when God was teaching me to love Him more and I would be joyful and there would be times when those on my life path would be the joyful ones and I wouldn't.

I had to learn very fast that my joy is what satan was after. The Joy of the salvation of the Lord! If the enemy could take that from me in whatever small way I might give in, then it would hold me back from doing what I was called to do for the Lord!

Oh, but Jesus!
Jesus! Jesus! Jesus!
My sweet and loving, always forgiving Jesus.
He is where my joy is found!

So today I want to challenge you to start this new year with remembrance of that joy. The joy that tastes like honey to your tongue. The joy that YOU are a precious child of God!

The joy that no matter how much you may have messed up, you are covered in the blood of the Lamb!

And if you've never experienced the sweetness of the joy of the Lord's salvation, then I encourage you once again to surrender to Jesus. Ask for Him to be the Lord and Savior of your life.

"If you confess with your mouth, "Jesus is Lord," and believe in your heart that God raised Him from the dead, you will be saved.

For everyone who calls on the name of the Lord will be saved."
Romans 10:9, 13 HCSB

Come see what goodness Jesus has for you!
Come remember what it was like when you first found that JOY!

And Let that joy be the theme for all you create in the new year!

You Have Victory

I wanted to send you all some encouragement this morning!

Sometimes our battles, our thoughts, and our situations seem so much bigger and scarier than we can handle. The enemy will tell us lies that will have us living in fear and unable to recognize God's voice in the midst of our trial.

But God's Word says differently. His word tells us that satan is the father of lies (*John 8:44*) and that we have not been given a spirit of fearfulness, but a spirit of power, love, and sound judgement. *(2 Timothy 1:7)*

If you are facing something that has you filled with fear, repeat that last Scripture over and over until it is embedded in your mind so strongly that nothing the enemy says can enter!

Fill your thoughts with God's Word.

God will never leave you, never forsake you and will always, always accept you.

When it feels like no one else loves you, my friend, listen carefully, Jesus does!

I love you ladies and I pray that today you will lay down your burdens at the feet of Jesus and worship Him.

Sit in His presence and rest!

"But thanks be to God, who gives us the victory through our Lord Jesus Christ! Therefore, my dear brothers, be steadfast, immovable, always excelling in the Lord's work, knowing that your labor in the Lord is not in vain."
1 Corinthians 15:57-58 HCSB

Baby Steps

Our lives are in constant change and growth. Sometimes, we get stuck in comfort and have a hard time moving in a new direction.

I'm learning every minute of the day, and I'm nowhere near perfect, but I can see God in action in my life, and that gives me hope!

It's amazing to look back over the past few months; giving up my businesses, my passions, my desires, all to seek after God's plan and His desires.

It's been a crazy journey so far and I have seen many moments of "growing pains" but I know that God has always and will always lead me to where He needs me.

The saying in this photo *(I'm learning to love the sound of my heels walking away from things not meant for me)* couldn't be any closer to the truth for me right now. It's a season of growing more and learning to walk away from what is not meant for me so that I can walk right into what is!

I am nothing without Jesus.

I can do nothing without Jesus.

I can be nothing without Jesus.

1 Corinthians 13 is my favorite chapter of the Bible. Not because of what it says love is but because it proves I am nothing without God's Love.

"If I speak human or angelic languages but do not have love, I am a sounding gong or a clanging cymbal. If I have the gift of prophecy and understand all mysteries and all knowledge, and if I have all faith so that I can move mountains but do not have love, I am nothing. And if I donate all my goods to feed the poor, and if I give my body in order to boast but do not have love, I gain nothing."
1 Corinthians 13:1-3 HCSB

Trusting and believing God to guide my steps. Even if I can only move one foot at a time in the darkness until I reach the light.

Here I am, Lord! Use me!

Encourage Her

God has blessed me with many wonderful women throughout my life. Some have been for only a season, others are in for the long haul, but each of them has impacted me and taught me to give, to love, to fight, to cherish, to motivate, and to encourage. I challenge every woman this reaches to choose another woman God has placed in your path and encourage them. Choose someone new every day! Give them a compliment. Help them grow their business. Pray with them. Hug them. Send them a gift. Show them love. We need more women of integrity and honor. We need more women who are strong and willing to move beyond society's belief that we must hate each other.

Every woman has been blessed with a talent. Some may share the same talents as you and others may have talents and gifts you only dream of having. But each and every one of our talents working together can impact the next generation of women to grow strong together. It's time we stop jealousy and hatred towards one another and start encouraging and uplifting the women we encounter. We must form our sisterhood, no one else is going to do it for us. Encourage another woman today, and another the day after that and the day after that....

Imagine a world full of women who encourage! It starts with YOU!

"Therefore encourage one another and build each other up as you are already doing."
1 Thessalonians 5:11 HCSB

Words Are Powerful

Look at the beginning of Genesis.
Genesis 1:3 Then God said...
Genesis 1:6 Then God said...
Genesis 1:9 Then God said...

Over and over you'll find those words in the book of Genesis as you read the creation of the earth, animals, people, and all things!

God spoke those things into existence!
If you have ever thought your words hold no power or no value, think again!
Our creator made us in His image. He spoke life into life!

What words are you choosing?
Words that create life or words that create death?

This week I spoke with a friend about how the simplest things we say might have the greatest impact in someone's life.

That impact can be good, or it can be bad.
We can plant seeds of encouragement or we can plant seeds of doubt.
So, the next time you open your mouth to speak, ask yourself which you are about to create?

Life or death.

Your words are powerful!
Choose them wisely!

Matthew 12:34

__Balancing Act__

Sometimes our problem and our solution lies in the shift of our perspective. Pleasing people can sound like this:

"Be bold for Jesus" ...not that bold.

"Obey the Lord's calling on your life" ...you're doing that for applause

"Follow Jesus and speak in truth and love" ...who are you to judge me?

You see no matter what you try to do to please people you will never find the balance and will fail according to man's standards.

But when you shift your focus from people to Jesus and follow only what Jesus asks of you and what His standards are, then, and only then can you continue to love people and walk with eyes on Jesus.

People will fail you, love them anyway.

Eyes on Jesus!

March forward for His glory, Soldier!

March forward!

"For am I now trying to win the favor of people, or God? Or am I striving to please people? If I were still trying to please people, I would not be a slave of Christ."
Galatians 1:10 HCSB

Beautiful Peace

While I was outside playing with Kainen and Ax I noticed these beautiful purple irises in my front yard! So gorgeous!

I looked at this flower and how beautiful it is, and it reminded me of these scriptures where Jesus is teaching not to worry about anything.

Actually, the title my bible gives these verses is "The Cure for Anxiety"

""This is why I tell you: Don't worry about your life, what you will eat or what you will drink; or about your body, what you will wear. Isn't life more than food and the body more than clothing? Look at the birds of the sky: They don't sow or reap or gather into barns, yet your heavenly Father feeds them. Aren't you worth more than they? Can any of you add a single cubit to his height by worrying? And why do you worry about clothes? Learn how the wildflowers of the field grow: they don't labor or spin thread. Yet I tell you that not even Solomon in all his splendor was adorned like one of these! If that's how God clothes the grass of the field, which is here today and thrown into the furnace tomorrow, won't He do much more for you — you of little faith? So don't worry, saying, 'What will we eat?' or 'What will we drink?' or 'What will we wear?' For the idolaters eagerly seek all these things, and your heavenly Father knows that you need

them. But seek first the kingdom of God and His righteousness, and all these things will be provided for you. Therefore don't worry about tomorrow, because tomorrow will worry about itself. Each day has enough trouble of its own."
Matthew 6:25-34 HCSB

Today alone I have received an unusual amount of private prayer requests about anxiety and worry. I know the Lord allowed me to be stopped in my tracks to gaze at this beautiful creation He made to remind you and I that He is still in control!

I pray in this moment you soak in the beauty of God's work around you. Choose to focus on seeking the kingdom of God first and know that if He clothes the fields in such beauty, then you, sweet friend, will be clothed in so much more.

He is Jehovah Jireh, Our Provider!

Praise and Glory and Honor and Blessings be to our Risen King, Our Savior, Our God!

Holy Spirit move upon the lives of those who read this message and bring them an immeasurable peace that can only come from the Great I Am!

In Jesus Christ's Name!

The Road to Endurance

*R*omans 12:12 says to be joyful in hope, patient in affliction and persistent in prayer.

As we are tested, trialed, and facing battles it's often hard to remember the importance of "patient in affliction".

The definition of affliction is something that causes pain or suffering. Words associated with affliction are distressed, torment, misery.

Thinking about times of affliction in my own life, it makes me cringe at the thought of being patient in them as well.

Exactly how can one be patient when the world seems to be caving in, when others appear to be stacked against you, when you are fighting one battle after another?

Our normal response is to fix the problem, to find a solution, a way out. We want to claw our way to safety! We sometimes begin to build walls of defense around our lives and our hearts. We search for the cure. We desperately seek for better than this moment. We make decisions based on feelings and emotions rather than on the guidance of the Holy Spirit. We want to attack, defend, guard and protect ourselves from the sting of rejection, loneliness, betrayal, hurt, and pain.

I'm reminded of Job in these trying times. The suffering he endured was unfathomable. He lost, and then lost more, and then lost even more.

I can't imagine the pain and the suffering! Pure Anguish! Then in his deepest, most painful moment his friends wrongfully accuse him and stand against him!

"My friends scoff at me as I weep before God."
Job 16:20

Being patient in affliction has to be one of the hardest, seemingly unbearable trials we know, but through this endurance is built.

Endurance is the ability to withstand wear and tear, or the capacity in which one handles a situation without giving up.

"For this very reason, make every effort to supplement your faith with goodness, goodness with knowledge, knowledge with self-control, self-control with endurance, endurance with godliness, godliness with brotherly affection, and brotherly affection with love. For if these qualities are yours and are increasing, they will keep you from being useless or unfruitful in the knowledge of our Lord Jesus Christ."
2 Peter 1:5-8

"Consider it a great joy, my brothers, whenever you experience various trials, knowing that the testing of your faith produces endurance."

James 1:2-3

The building up of endurance can only happen by being stretched and pushed to our limits over and over. Each time our limit is stretched it reaches a new level. With each new level our endurance grows. As our endurance grows we become stronger, more prepared for the next punch.

Think of it this way, consider your job. We can use any job; being a mom, a hair stylist, a CEO, a doctor, a teacher. Put your "job" in the blank here.

When you began you were not at the same level you are now. You had to learn by schooling or experiences. You have been tested, failed, grown, and stretched to your limits and because of those moments you can now call yourself professional, experienced, mature, or recognized in your field.

Through patience during our afflictions, we gain endurance, and endurance allows us to overcome more than we thought possible.

If you are in a season of affliction, embrace it with patience, knowing your endurance will be built, you will be stronger, and you will overcome! Because He who is in you is greater than He who is in the world!

"You are from God, little children, and you have conquered them, because the One who is in you is greater than the one who is in the world."

1 John 4:4

Juicy Fruit

Kainen and I had a conversation this morning about the difference in what the world wants to offer us vs what God wants to offer us.

Shortly after a dear friend shared a page from her devotion.

It made me think.

The enemy will make many things that are evil appear to be good for you. Be careful in searching for power and titles, they will come both with great responsibility and great loss.

I love where the devotion says, "they all have the same ending...futility." Another word for futility is fruitlessness. And we are told to not only produce fruit, but good fruit. Reminds me of *Matthew 13.*

Is what you are seeking after today going to matter in a year? a decade? a lifetime from now?

Keep your mind and eyes focused on producing good fruit, not power or selfish ambitions.

""I am the vine; you are the branches. The one who remains in Me and I in him produces much fruit, because you can do nothing without Me."
John 15:5 HCSB

"Now the works of the flesh are obvious: sexual immorality, moral impurity, promiscuity, idolatry, sorcery, hatreds, strife, jealousy, outbursts of anger, selfish ambitions, dissensions, factions, envy, drunkenness, carousing, and anything similar. I tell you about these things in advance — as I told you before — that those who practice such things will not inherit the kingdom of God. But the fruit of the Spirit is love, joy, peace, patience, kindness, goodness, faith, gentleness, self-control. Against such things there is no law."
Galatians 5:19-23 HCSB

Are You Tired of Fighting?

Women are in a constant battle to reach the top of the mountain; trying to outdo another's talent, working tirelessly to be the best of what someone else was called to be, and all the while completely missing the magnificent creation God intended them to become.

There's a lot thrown at us as women; lots of comparing ourselves to others, and lots of competing with one another.

We claw our way to the top, only to find it to be the loneliest of places. We see one woman being successful in a particular area, become envious, and then work to mimic her accomplishments in hopes we too will become successful.

But that isn't how God designed things for each of us. We are many parts working as one body.

"Show family affection to one another with brotherly love. Outdo one another in showing honor."
Romans 12:10 HCSB

"Now as we have many parts in one body, and all the parts do not have the same function, in the same way we who are many are one body in Christ and individually members of one another."
Romans 12:4-5 HCSB

If all we ever do is seek to accomplish the same goal as what another woman has been called to, then we stay in the same position, never allowing motion to exist and to move us forward in God's purpose.

God does not need twenty of the same woman. He doesn't even need two of the same! He needs us individually discovering our gifts and talents and making those work together, not against one another. Fighting against God's plan will never lead you anywhere, but moving in the direction of obedience to God, will.

"And this is love: that we walk according to His commands. This is the command as you have heard it from the beginning: you must walk in love."
2 John 1:6 HCSB

Let today be the day you stop seeking after being like, looking like, acting like, and mimicking another woman and become the woman who discovers the beauty, truth, and skill God has placed in you to create a powerful means to give Him glory. You don't need to be like everyone else. You simply need to be you.

It's time we stop the war against one another, stop allowing your time to be wasted by the enemy's tactics. It's time to stop fighting with her and start discovering you.

You won't answer for her calling. You'll answer for yours.

Be who He needs YOU to be!

You were created for greatness! You were designed with purpose!

"He has made everything beautiful in its time. Also He has put eternity in their hearts, except that no one can find out the work that God does from beginning to end."
Ecclesiastes 3:11 NKJV

You may only see the success of another woman and may never know the hardships, heartaches, failures, and disappointments it took her facing to get her to where God is using her now.

The amount of punches she has endured many may not be willing to go through to get to the place where she is serving, yet many covet what she has, whether tangible or intangible things.

"A tranquil heart is life to the body, but jealousy is rottenness to the bones."
Proverbs 14:30 HCSB

Don't envy anyone; their story may not have always been as perfect as it appears to be from the only view you have seen it from.

There is purpose in our individuality. Find that purpose in yourself and then work with others who have done the same and grow the Kingdom of God, together!

We can all climb the mountain simultaneously, but instead of stepping on the fingers of another woman to cause her to stumble and lose grip, reach for her hand and lift her up to the top with you.

<u>Unity</u>

I woke up this morning to a text from my sister. I smiled. I'm thankful for people like her in my life who encourage me; those who love me in good moments and help me grow in bad moments, the ones who I know have my back no matter what; not to just "be on my side" and defend me, but to help me stay on track with Christ.

It's hard to lose people. I don't mean losing them because their life is over, rather losing them because they walk away.

It's painful to once know someone and have shared a personal relationship with them and then one day you realize things have changed, you've drifted apart, or a hurtful moment has caused division.

The enemy likes to work that way. He wins when he can "divide and conquer". But Christ teaches us unity. When you see division happening in a Christian relationship, friendship, church, or family, recognize this as the enemy at work.

It isn't people you are fighting with, Ephesians 6 very clearly says that. It's the power and principalities of the darkness.

It's painful to lose those you love, to be ridiculed, talked about, when lies are told and hearts are hardened. It's very painful.

God calls us to reconcile with one another, but when that doesn't happen, what do you do?

You pray! You put on the armor of God. You continue to love as if no one has ever hurt you before.

Losing people is hard. It's scary. It's painful.

Pray for those who walk away.

I also imagine Christ feels the same about us when we walk away from Him. Have you walked away? Ask for forgiveness and turn your face back to the Father.

Love covers a multitude of sins.

Find unity in Jesus.

"Therefore I, the prisoner for the Lord, urge you to walk worthy of the calling you have received, with all humility and gentleness, with patience, accepting one another in love, diligently keeping the unity of the Spirit with the peace that binds us. There is one body and one Spirit — just as you were called to one hope at your calling — one Lord, one faith, one baptism, one God and Father of all, who is above all and through all and in all."
Ephesians 4:1-6 HCSB

Hidden

I have to share this with y'all because it is too amazing not to!

As you know, if you watched me live this morning on the devotion, I had an eye doctor appointment.

As I was waiting on Kainen to get dressed he walks through the living room and sees $40 perfectly folded on floor. None of us ever have cash on us but we did have a few visitors this week, so I contacted them. It belongs to none of them. I asked Jeremy to be certain it wasn't his and he said no.

Let me emphasize here that we (Jeremy, Kainen and I) walked by this particular place where the money was a total of about 20 times or more, plus since we've had visitors last the floor has been swept clean twice. My point, there was no money there and then there was money there. I can't make this stuff up!

I put the money in my pocket and off to the doctor's office I went. I figured God would let me know when or what to do with it.

I had decided in an effort to save money I would only get contacts or glasses this time not both. I decided contacts, since the glasses I have (although years old) work fine and I would much rather have my contacts, so I can wear sunglasses while driving.

I arrive at the doctor, he examines my eyes, places drops in to dilate my pupils and sends me to the waiting room.

The nice lady who works in the front office helped me choose my frames that I thought I would pick out now but purchase later.

She tells me the frame cost, the lens cost, and then taxes.

My total: $41.80

Yep! All I could think about was our devotion from Monday, Jehovah Jireh!

Our Lord will provide. Today for me it was a pair of glasses. Who knows what blessings are heading your way! Trust in Him! Follow His path! He is watching, listening, and providing in ways that are unexplainable and unthinkable to our minds!

"And my God will supply all your needs according to His riches in glory in Christ Jesus."
Philippians 4:19 HCSB

Sea Sick

The last few weeks the word anxiety has come up in many conversations. I've talked with friends who are anxious, I've talked with family members who are anxious, I've even been anxious myself!

I noticed a common thread in every conversation about anxiety; the fear was coming from a place of doubt.

It got me thinking about this night described in scripture.

"As He got into the boat, His disciples followed Him. Suddenly, a violent storm arose on the sea, so that the boat was being swamped by the waves. But He was sleeping. So the disciples came and woke Him up, saying, "Lord, save us! We're going to die!" But He said to them, "Why are you fearful, you of little faith?" Then He got up and rebuked the winds and the sea. And there was a great calm. The men were amazed and asked, "What kind of man is this? — even the winds and the sea obey Him!"

Matthew 8:23-27 HCSB

The disciples have just witnessed miracle after miracle. A man was healed from a skin disease, a servant healed from paralysis, and even Peter's mother in law was healed from fever!

After all of those miracles occurred many who were demon possessed were brought to Jesus and healed.

After seeing these miracles, surely, the disciples would have strong faith in Jesus!

Right?

Wrong.

The next events that unfold are eerily scary!

Picture this for a moment: it's dark, it's storming, and they are on a boat surrounded by water! That's enough terror for one night!

This storm wasn't a gentle breeze and a little rain either! It's described as a raging storm! A fierce windstorm that was tossing waves that were breaking over the boat! The disciples were scared!!

S. C. A. R. E. D.

Anxiety! Fear! Terror!

All the while Jesus is sleeping!

Why isn't He worried while this storm rages against the boat?

"Doesn't He care?" (The disciples asked Him.)

He isn't worried because He knows He holds the authority over the storm!

Jesus got up and said, "Be still!" And guess what happened? The wind obeyed Him! The sea quieted!

Aren't we the same as the disciples when we focus on the wind and the storms of our lives?!

We become so full of anxiety that we forget all the miracles we've witnessed our Savior perform!

That's the tactic of the enemy! To make us forget the truth of Jesus!

He knows we are sealed by the Holy Spirit so the enemy uses every fiery dart he can to make us forget the power in Jesus!

Scripture tells us the enemy comes to kill, steal and destroy but that Jesus came to give life abundantly!!

So, the next time you are faced with anxiety, recognize the enemy's tactic and remember that your storm has to obey the authority of Jesus Christ! The power within your storm is remembering you are an overcomer in Christ!

He has already won your battles!

Tonight, I pray you rest in that truth!

Let's Get Real

Today, I'm tired.
I'm worn out.
Mostly from daily activities; the normal routine of life, battling health issues, doctor visits and appointments, cooking, cleaning, homeschool teaching, running errands, having a never ending to do lists. Exhausted from worry, stress, anxiety. You could say I'm feeling a bit emptied; a bit weary. Then there's spiritual struggles; fighting against my flesh, wanting to defend myself in situations where I'm falsely accused, trying to seek after God's plan and feeling slammed against the wall time and again, a bit scattered about, needing direction.

"When He saw the crowds, He felt compassion for them, because they were weary and worn out, like sheep without a shepherd."
Matthew 9:36 HCSB

I imagine this is what Jesus saw as He and the disciples looked upon the crowds that followed.
Real people.
Real struggles.
Real worries.
Real pain.
Their faces dirty and wet with tears. Their eyebrows furrowed from immense pain. Their hearts breaking.

80

Their eyes piercing into His face yearning for relief and hope.

Let's look at the whole story
"Then Jesus went to all the towns and villages, teaching in their synagogues, preaching the good news of the kingdom, and healing every disease and every sickness. When He saw the crowds, He felt compassion for them, because they were weary and worn out, like sheep without a shepherd. Then He said to His disciples, "The harvest is abundant, but the workers are few. Therefore, pray to the Lord of the harvest to send out workers into His harvest.""
Matthew 9:35-38 HCSB

Jesus has been walking from place to place seeing people like this. People like us. Feeling alone, hurt, unloved, sick and needing, desperately desiring someone to save them!
Scripture says "like sheep without a shepherd"
Picture what that would look like with me for a moment.
A flock of sheep wandering about looking for water, green pastures, shelter from storms and protection from enemies.
Wandering with no guidance, no direction, no hope.

Some days this is what I feel like. This is what I imagine the crowds following Jesus felt like.

And then I'm reminded by God's word, that I am no longer the lost sheep. I know who my Savior is, who my Shepherd is! He is Jehovah-Raah! The Lord My Shepherd!

"My sheep hear My voice, I know them, and they follow Me."
John 10:27 HCSB

I know the voice of my Savior!

I know when to follow!

I may not always want to do things His way, but that's the choice you must make to obey the Shepherd!

I know when He sees me, He has compassion!

I know He will guide me to water, to green pastures, shield me from my storms and protect me from my enemies!

And then I am reminded of part two:

The harvest is plenty, but the workers are few! Pray for workers!

So, I remember my Shepherd's calling for me, and I allow Him to restore my strength, because someone out there needs to see the Hope of Jesus Christ in me.

Friend, someone needs to see the Hope of Jesus Christ in you!

He sees that you're weary and worn!

He knows exactly how you need to be restored and strengthened!

And He still needs you to be a light!

The Student and The Teacher

This month we are going to walk step by step through the book of Joshua. Exploring every moment of opportunity to learn and form a deeper understanding of God and His promises.

Moses had been told by God in *Numbers 27* that Joshua would be his successor.

The book of Joshua begins with the Israelites having completed the mourning of Moses' death and God speaking to Joshua.

God speaks encouragement to him over and over; "I will be with you" "I will never forsake you" "do not be afraid" "be strong and courageous".

We read many words of encouragement to Joshua from our Lord as He prepares him for the job ahead.

I love verse 5.
"No one will be able to stand against you as long as you live. I will be with you, just as I was with Moses. I will not leave you or forsake you."
Joshua 1:5 HCSB

God has just confirmed Joshua's calling and given him a promise to cling to that He (God) will be with him (Joshua) the whole way just like He was with Moses.

I think about how Joshua must have felt in this moment. Can you even fathom leading God's people into the promised land?

The amount of stress and pressure Joshua must have been feeling would be enough to make me crumble.

Joshua has spent so much time with Moses leading the Israelites, but this was now the time for him to take his position of leadership.

Leadership is something I believe we are all called in to when we surrender our lives to Jesus. We each have been told to go and make disciples *(Matthew 28:19)*, which makes us leaders, right?

This also reminds me of the promise that God will never leave us. He will equip us with everything we need, every person we need to learn from, and every opportunity to succeed in His mission for us!

My challenge to you is to answer these questions as we journey with Joshua:

1. Who is your leader? Who in your life are you observing? Are the people you surround yourself with supporting you, teaching you and guiding you to take the position God has placed you in?

2. Who are you leading? Who in your life are you helping to grow in Christ? Are your actions replicant of Christ and of a godly leader?

Moses prepared Joshua, Joshua learned how to lead the Israelites, and in the midst of all of it there was God fulfilling His promises!

Where are you right now?
Moses or Joshua?
Leading or learning?

Both positions are necessary and important.
Neither one is better than the other.
Find the value in where you are and cling to the promise that God is with you through your journey!

Blessed Assurance

Good morning sweet friends! I am taking the rest of the week to rest and relax so we won't have devotions live again until Monday. In the meantime, I want to encourage you to read the resurrection story, be familiar with it entirely and share it with someone or with many over the rest of this week. This week represents the very reason we call ourselves Christians, followers of Jesus!

Matthew 27-28
Mark 15-16
Luke 23-24
John 19-20

Let's share the story of the truth of Christ!
Share the blessed assurance you have been freely given!

This is my story, this is my song!

A little history about the song blessed assurance:
"Blessed Assurance" is a well-known Christian hymn. The lyrics were written in 1873 by blind hymn writer Fanny Crosby to the music written in 1873 by Phoebe Knapp.

Share your story, share His story!

You Are Powerful in Christ!

Yesterday I had a moment of realization of power within my reach!

Not power that I have myself, but the power that I have through Jesus Christ.

We experienced bad weather that was producing tornados, and in the midst of those storms, I found myself terrified.

The meteorologist talked about the storm getting closer and closer and as it approached my town it was building into a much larger storm than expected.

We had already gone to our storm shelter, but as I stood at the doorway and watched as the wind increased, the lighting seemed closer and closer and the rain was heavier,

I began praying, "Lord, protect us!"

Every few minutes an update would be given by the news and the storm would be closer and larger than before.

And in that moment right before I knew the storm would be hitting my small community, I remembered my Jesus power!

You see, I had prayed for protection, but I forgot that Jesus Christ gave me the same power He had on this Earth!

And if I had authority in the name of Jesus Christ to do as He did, and if Jesus calmed a storm, if He told it to obey and it listened, then in His name this storm had to listen too!

And you know what I saw, I began to see the wind calm, the lightning cease, and the rain slack. That's the power of Jesus Christ!

You know, we all have moments of fear, when we feel we've lost all control of things, when we need peace, calmness and serenity.

Let's not forget that the God who made the earth also gave us a way out of our storms!

Sister, your storm may be bigger than you, but it is not bigger than our Jesus.

You have power and authority in the name of Jesus! Today, I encourage you to be strong in the Lord and overcome those storms!

"I will give you the keys of the kingdom of heaven, and whatever you bind on earth is already bound in heaven, and whatever you loose on earth is already loosed in heaven.""
Matthew 16:19 HCSB

"On that day, when evening had come, He told them, "Let's cross over to the other side of the sea." So they left the crowd and took Him along since He was already in the boat. And other boats were with Him. A fierce windstorm arose, and the waves were breaking over the boat, so that the boat was already being swamped. But He was in the stern, sleeping on the cushion. So they woke Him up and said to Him, "Teacher! Don't You care

that we're going to die? " He got up, rebuked the wind, and said to the sea, "Silence! Be still! " The wind ceased, and there was a great calm. Then He said to them, "Why are you fearful? Do you still have no faith? " And they were terrified and asked one another, "Who then is this? Even the wind and the sea obey Him! ""

   Mark 4:35-41 HCSB

"Then Jesus came near and said to them, "All authority has been given to Me in heaven and on earth."

   Matthew 28:18 HCSB

""I assure you: The one who believes in Me will also do the works that I do. And he will do even greater works than these, because I am going to the Father. Whatever you ask in My name, I will do it so that the Father may be glorified in the Son. If you ask Me anything in My name, I will do it."

   John 14:12-14 HCSB

Do You Hear Me Knocking?

I've often wondered how many times I've heard God knocking but didn't answer Him.

Or how many times has someone else knocked on my door and yet I didn't hear them either.

Not literally knocked but reached out to me for help, cried out to me for advice or attention or love!

I'm sure we have all faced times that we haven't answered someone's call. Maybe we weren't paying attention, maybe we were being self- centered, or maybe we simply distracted by other things. Thankfully, we have a God who tells us to continually knock and He will answer us!

If we seek knowledge, He tells us He will give us great things that we can't even comprehend!

He tells us in His word that those who ask will receive and those who search will find and for those who knock the door will be opened.

Being persistent is key to receiving our answer.

No matter what we are seeking from God:

a deeper relationship, the right answer, healing, or clarity, He will answer us if we will continue to seek Him.

Today, I encourage you to dig deep, be persistent in your knocking, stay aware, remain faithful in prayer until the door is opened and your answers are delivered!

Your prayers are heard, and our Father has spoken that He will answer. Don't ever give up searching for Him!

"Call to Me and I will answer you and tell you great and incomprehensible things you do not know."
Jeremiah 33:3 HCSB

"For everyone who asks receives, and the one who searches finds, and to the one who knocks, the door will be opened."
Matthew 7:8 HCSB

"He also said to them: "Suppose one of you has a friend and goes to him at midnight and says to him, 'Friend, lend me three loaves of bread, because a friend of mine on a journey has come to me, and I don't have anything to offer him.' Then he will answer from inside and say, 'Don't bother me! The door is already locked, and my children and I have gone to bed. I can't get up to give you anything.' I tell you, even though he won't get up and give him anything because he is his friend, yet because of his friend's persistence, he will get up and give him as much as he needs. "So, I say to you, keep asking, and it will be given to you. Keep searching, and you will find. Keep knocking, and the door will be opened to you. For everyone who asks receives, and the one who searches finds, and to the one who knocks, the door will be opened. What father among you, if his son asks for a fish, will give him a snake instead of a fish? Or if he asks for an egg, will

give him a scorpion? If you then, who are evil, know how to give good gifts to your children, how much more will the heavenly Father give the Holy Spirit to those who ask Him?""

Luke 11:5-13 HCSB

Are You Keeping Good Company?

At some point in our lives each of us has needed a friend; someone we can lean on, someone who would encourage us, someone to giggle with and someone who would pray with us.

But have you checked your friendships lately?

Do they mimic a friendship with Christ?

Does your friend talk with you about Jesus?

Are they uplifting and encouraging?

Many times, we get lost inside our very closest relationships with others that we don't realize Christ isn't present in them!

You may feel like what seemed to be a great friendship isn't necessarily the best friendship for you at the moment.

It's a hard place to come to in the road of deciding which direction to take when we begin our relationship with Christ. But thankfully as always God provides the answers we need in His word!

Walk closely with Him every day! Build your relationship with Him. Read His word! Ask for His guidance and you will begin to see true friendships unfold; real heart felt love being poured out in your relationships.

Ask God if who you are hanging out with is advancing or hindering your walk with Him and if you are being a true Christ like friend to others!

"Do not be deceived: "Bad company corrupts good morals."" 1 Corinthians 15:33 HCSB

"A man with many friends may be harmed, but there is a friend who stays closer than a brother."
Proverbs 18:24 HCSB

""As the Father has loved Me, I have also loved you. Remain in My love. If you keep My commands you will remain in My love, just as I have kept My Father's commands and remain in His love. "I have spoken these things to you so that My joy may be in you and your joy may be complete. This is My command: Love one another as I have loved you. No one has greater love than this, that someone would lay down his life for his friends. You are My friends if you do what I command you. I do not call you slaves anymore, because a slave doesn't know what his master is doing. I have called you friends, because I have made known to you everything I have heard from My Father. You did not choose Me, but I chose you. I appointed you that you should go out and produce fruit and that your fruit should remain, so that whatever you ask the Father in My name, He will give you. This is what I command you: Love one another."
John 15:9-17 HCSB

Quiet Time

Jesus gives us many examples showing the importance of quiet time with our Father.

I think a lot about how perfect it would be to never have to do anything but talk and walk with Christ! And then I'm reminded again that I will have that opportunity one day in heaven with Him. But for now, it is so easy to let the daily distractions of this life take that precious, intimate time away from me and my Jesus!

We often get so completely engulfed with our daily routines we forget God needs and longs for our attention, too! Our lives can be consumed with work, being wives, being mothers, taking care of our family, our friends, our neighbors; we even neglect our quiet time with the Lord for church activities.

Yes, it is so easy to get caught up in doing and being busy for the Lord that we forget to speak to and listen to the Lord!

When is the last time you set aside true, genuine quiet time with God? Just like your earthly relationships need nurturing and attention and intimacy, so does and even more so does our relationship with Christ need the same.

Let today's scriptures remind us to cherish our quiet time with our Father, more than we treasure the things of this earth and our fleshly needs.

Somebody please, take me to the King!

"Then Jesus was led up by the Spirit into the wilderness to be tempted by the Devil. After He had fasted 40 days and 40 nights, He was hungry. Then the tempter approached Him and said, "If You are the Son of God, tell these stones to become bread." But He answered, "It is written: Man must not live on bread alone but on every word that comes from the mouth of God." Then the Devil took Him to the holy city, had Him stand on the pinnacle of the temple, and said to Him, "If You are the Son of God, throw Yourself down. For it is written: He will give His angels orders concerning you, and they will support you with their hands so that you will not strike your foot against a stone." Jesus told him, "It is also written: Do not test the Lord your God." Again, the Devil took Him to a very high mountain and showed Him all the kingdoms of the world and their splendor. And he said to Him, "I will give You all these things if You will fall down and worship me." Then Jesus told him, "Go away, Satan! For it is written: Worship the Lord your God, and serve only Him." Then the Devil left Him, and immediately angels came and began to serve Him."
Matthew 4:1-11 HCSB

"Then Jesus came with them to a place called Gethsemane, and He told the disciples, "Sit here while I go over there and pray.""
Matthew 26:36 HCSB

The Voice of Truth

It is easy to feel overwhelmed by all the voices we hear daily.

With so many voices coming at us, it sometimes becomes hard to recognize God's voice vs the voice of the enemy.

It's important that we understand how to take time to listen and recognize God's voice.

The enemy wants us to hear his untruth, his lies, and deceit.

But the Holy Spirit, The Voice of Truth is much stronger if we first learn to listen and accept it!

God wants to lead us into the gracious and loving plan He has designed. God's voice will never lead us astray.

The Voice of truth will always lead you to Jesus not away from Jesus.

father's desires. He was a murderer from the beginning and has not stood in the truth, because there is no truth in him. When he tells a lie, he speaks from his own nature, because he is a liar and the father of liars. *(John 8:44 HCSB)*

"For I know the plans I have for you" — *this is the Lord's declaration* — *"plans for your welfare, not for disaster, to give you a future and a hope."*
Jeremiah 29:11 HCSB

"God is not a man who lies, or a son of man who changes His mind. Does He speak and not act, or promise and not fulfill?"
   Numbers 23:19 HCSB

Contact Information

To book Andrea Kellum as a guest speaker, email:
info@andreakellum.com

To join the Coffee and Jesus devotion group on facebook go to:
https://www.facebook.com/groups/166846717211514/

For more information on other available books, devotions, and Women's bible studies by Andrea Kellum please visit:
www.andreakellum.com

Mailing Address:
Andrea Kellum
Changing Crowns Ministries
P.O. Box 314
Woodstock, Alabama 35188

Follow on Social Media:
Facebook: www.facebook.com/changingcrownsministries
Instagram: www.instagram.com/andrea_kellum